My New GLASSES

How My Favorite Frames Help Me See

Written by Helena Haraštová
Illustrated by Ana Kobern

Sky Pony Press
New York

First published as *Hurray, I Wear Glasses*
© Designed by B4U Publishing,
member of Albatros Media Group, 2022.
Author: Helena Haraštová.
Illustrator: Ana Kobern.
www.albatrosmedia.eu
All rights reserved.

First Sky Pony Press edition, 2024

Sky Pony Press books may be purchased in bulk at special discounts for sales promotion, corporate gifts, fund-raising, or educational purposes. Special editions can also be created to specifications. For details, contact the Special Sales Department, Sky Pony Press, 307 West 36th Street, 11th Floor, New York, NY 10018 or info@skyhorsepublishing.com.

Sky Pony® is a registered trademark of Skyhorse Publishing, Inc.®, a Delaware corporation.

Visit our website at www.skyponypress.com.

10 9 8 7 6 5 4 3 2 1

Manufactured in China, January 2024
This product conforms to CPSIA 2008

Library of Congress Cataloging-in-Publication Data is available on file.

Cover design by B4U Publishing, member of Albatros Media Group
Cover illustrations by Ana Kobern
US Edition edited by Nicole Frail

Print ISBN: 978-1-5107-7857-3
Ebook ISBN: 978-1-5107-7858-0

CONTENTS

Introduction 2
What happens in your eyes? 4
At the ophthalmologist's 6
How do glasses work? 8
With glasses 9
Blind past 10
Wow, I can see! 12
Glasses for everyone 14
How to choose the right glasses 16
Famous visually impaired people 18
Glasses of the future 20
Challenging days 22
Looking after our eyes 24
Vision in the animal kingdom 26
We wear glasses – that's fantastic! 28

INTRODUCTION

Hello, my name's Joe, and I wear glasses. One day I noticed that I cannot see houses, trees, or my friends on the opposite side of the street very clearly. It felt like looking through a fogged window — but there was no window! I couldn't count birds on a branch or tell the numbers on the buses that went past me.

Hi, I'm Kitty, and I wear glasses, too. I've had my specs since I can remember. When I put them down, everything around me suddenly gets blurry and confusing. Objects that are far away from me are the only things I can see clearly.

How Joe sees the world.

How Kitty sees the world.

When Joe and Kitty put on their glasses, the world becomes alright again!

Did an eye doctor tell you to start wearing glasses, too? Maybe you're worried now – that the glasses will feel uncomfortable on your nose, that you'll look foolish, that other kids will mock you…. We know exactly what it's like! We were worried, too. But you can rest assured. In this book, we will show you everything you'll need to know about glasses, and in the end, you'll be proud to have them on your nose!

3

WHAT HAPPENS IN YOUR EYES?

- - - - - - - - - - - - - - - -

When healthy, all people's eyes work in the same way. All the parts of the eye play as a team, helping us see things properly.

A Light rays reflected from the things around you enter your eyeballs through the cornea and lens.

A

B

C

B Then they meet on a single point in the back of your eye, on the retina.

C From here, the optic nerves carry the message to the brain, which decides what we are actually looking at.

This is a complicated process. It's no wonder it sometimes goes wrong and various vision impairments appear. Did you notice that Joe's problem is different from Kitty's?

Far-sightedness

Kitty can see people and things that are far away from her without difficulties, but anything up close, such as the boxes she is peering at, look fuzzy to her. Kitty is **far-sighted** (a.k.a. long-sighted). That is because the light in her eyeball comes together behind the retina.

Near-sightedness

Joe can see people and things clearly if they are up close, but anything far away, such as friends on the other side of the street, look fuzzy to him. Joe is **near-sighted** (a.k.a. short-sighted). This is because the light rays in his eyeball come together before touching the retina.

Other vision impairments

Some people see things around them more or less blurry, no matter how near or far they are. (This eye problem is called **astigmatism**.) Sometimes one eye looks in the wrong direction, so the person sees double or has problems with spatial orientation. (This is called **strabismus**.) And some eye defects appear only later in life, as the eye grows older and loses its quickness and efficiency — that is why so many grannies and grandpas need reading glasses.

AT THE OPHTHALMOLOGIST'S

An ophthalmologist is an eye doctor who can tell how clearly you can see using all sorts of tests and exams.

He or she is able to identify any eye defect even before you notice something is wrong! The sooner a problem is discovered, the greater is the chance of fixing it.

How can the doctor know?

The doctor will test how the muscles in your eye work, how the light travels inside your eyeball, and if you can see everything properly. The ophthalmologist will see how different parts of your eye work together.

When Joe couldn't see very well, we took him to an ophthalmologist.

What will the eye doctor do?

At first, the ophthalmologist will ask all sorts of questions related to your vision before starting to check your eyes. With various tools, special glasses, and pictures, they will find out if your eyes work exactly as they should. You don't have to worry, because the doctor will always tell you what to do. For example, you will tell them what you can see on a board placed at some distance in the room, cover one eye with your hand, or look up or into the beam of the doctor's little flashlight.

Let's go early

Kitty went for a big eye exam when she was just a little toddler. Both of her parents wear glasses, and they know that many vision defects run in the family; children whose relatives suffer from sight problems often have them too. The ophthalmologist actually discovered a problem in Kitty's eyes, and the little girl's life hugely improved after she started wearing glasses. People should have their eyes checked even if they think their vision is good, because they often do not realize that they can't see so well. Did you know that even little babies have their eyes checked? Sometimes this helps find and fix a defect that would later make the child's life difficult.

HOW DO GLASSES WORK?

Joe and Kitty need to wear glasses to see the world clearly, nicely, and in the smallest detail. Maybe you are also getting used to your first glasses right now. How does this thing on your nose actually work?

The glasses (or spectacles) are usually specially adjusted just for your eyes, so that the glass or plastic helps your **lenses** and **corneas** correctly process everything that you look at. Thanks to glasses, the light entering your eyeball falls onto the very right spot on the **retina**.

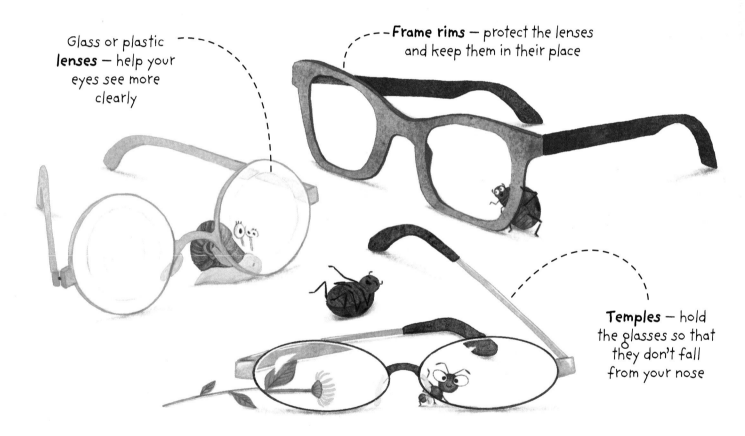

Glass or plastic **lenses** — help your eyes see more clearly

Frame rims — protect the lenses and keep them in their place

Temples — hold the glasses so that they don't fall from your nose

Some glasses have lenses with irregular thickness — those help people with **astigmatism** see everything perfectly clearly.

Sometimes the glass is the thinnest in the middle — this helps the **near-sighted** people see things that are far away.

But in other types of glasses, the middle part of the lenses is the thickest — those help the **far-sighted** people see things that are up close.

WITH GLASSES ...

... you will never get on a wrong bus!

... you won't overlook a friend across the street!

... you won't stumble, hit anything, or fall over so easily, because you will see any obstacle in time!

... you will never miss the target!

... you won't have headaches!

... you will easily count all the little things!

BLIND PAST

Joe, Kitty, and millions of other people who wear glasses sometimes wonder what our ancestors did in times when glasses had not yet been invented. What do you think?

Vision at times past and present

In the past, eye defects such as near-sightedness, far-sightedness, or astigmatism were quite rare — certainly less common than today. Why? People spent most of their time outdoors, and their eyes did not suffer from artificial light or computer screens. Those things have negative effects on human vision, and in modern times, we spend more and more time with them. Scientists believe that by 2050, more than half of the people on our planet will be near-sighted!

When a defect is not a defect at all

If some of our ancestors did have a vision impairment, they usually didn't really care. For most of their activities, they didn't need perfect vision, and they could easily adapt to their impaired sight. If far-sighted, they could become good hunters, and if near-sighted, they could sew clothes or decorate pottery. In the Middle Ages, near-sighted people were even sought-after as scribes, because their vision did not deteriorate by peering into manuscript pages, and they could work for many years.

The first tools

The very first vision-improving aid, a predecessor of glasses, was invented in India as early as the fifth century BC, but it became more famous in the Roman times. For reading, the Romans used a special glass that looked a bit like the magnifying glass we use today and worked basically the same way. The readers had to hold the glass in their hand.

From books to eye defects

As time went on, and more people learned to read and write, near-sightedness became more widely spread. The human eye can learn and adapt to what it needs most — so as people spent more time reading and writing, their vision got better for things up close but worsened for objects far away. This continues to happen even today — TV and computer screens or books give us not just entertainment and education, but also vision impairments. This is the price we pay for our comfortable lifestyle.

The dark side of blindness

While minor sight defects were rare in the old times compared to in our modern world, people in the past sometimes suffered from serious eye diseases and blindness. If a person lost sight altogether, there was no help available. Such people had trouble walking, became a burden for their families, and their handicap often made them grumpy and nasty. Nomadic tribes, for which a slow-walking individual was a threat, even left their blind members behind or killed them right away.

WOW, I CAN SEE!

Based on old Arabic texts, people in the thirteenth century in northern Italy invented **the first real glasses**. You can imagine what a hit they became! Those first specs were used only for reading, because people had to hold them in place or secure them by a peg, but even so, many, especially the monks, could not imagine life without them. The rims were made of wood, leather, or horn.

Before long, glasses became a symbol of **education and riches**. They were a must for all the wealthy and noble people in Europe, and soon the Silk Road brought them as far as Asia. Artists made beautiful rims decorated by hand. In China, too, spectacles were linked to high social status. Some judges were made to wear them to look more dignified!

1700

The year 1700 brought a true revolution in the history of glasses! People started making glasses with side hitches or **temples**. Suddenly, you didn't have to hold glasses on your nose with one hand, so you could wear them all day long. What a relief!

1750

After 1750, the Englishman **Benjamin Martin** became a famous maker of spectacles. He started making steel eye wires, into which he put thinner lenses than before. His specs became bestsellers, as every rich person wanted to have them.

1784

Another Benjamin, this time an American named Franklin, presented the very first **bifocal glasses** in 1784 – their upper part helped distance vision, while the bottom part enabled the wearer to see clearly up close. How did he make them? He cut two lenses in half, fitting them in a single rim! Bifocal glasses are still used today – but they are no longer made of old specs.

Benjamin Franklin

The turbulent nineteenth century brought some huge changes to the world. One of them was that many poorer people were now able to afford glasses, which were being made at large scale in **factories** and became cheaper. The most popular types included **folding spectacles** that you could wear in your pocket or special theater glasses hidden in a fan.

1862

But what good would all those wonderful inventions be if we didn't use them correctly? Until 1862, people chose their glasses at random from itinerant sellers. However, Doctor Herman Snellen from the Netherlands **invented a chart** with different-sized letters that helped him find out exactly which glasses his patients needed.

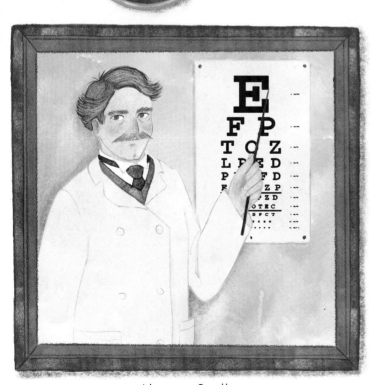

Herman Snellen

GLASSES FOR EVERYONE

- -

Today we are very lucky. Not only do we have glasses for all kinds of eye defects, but we can choose from a vast number of products so we get the pair that we like most, that fits the shape of our face, that matches our favorite colors, or even a pair for special occasions!

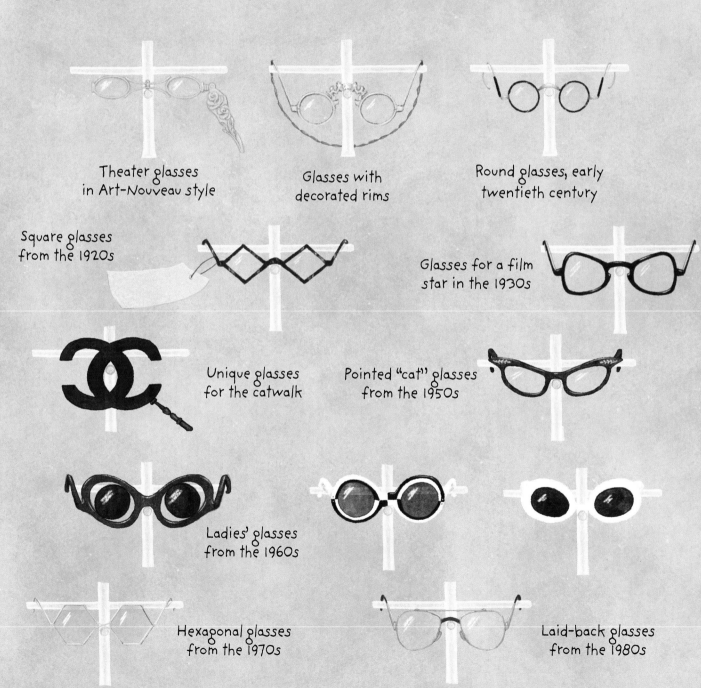

Theater glasses
in Art-Nouveau style

Glasses with
decorated rims

Round glasses, early
twentieth century

Square glasses
from the 1920s

Glasses for a film
star in the 1930s

Unique glasses
for the catwalk

Pointed "cat" glasses
from the 1950s

Ladies' glasses
from the 1960s

Hexagonal glasses
from the 1970s

Laid-back glasses
from the 1980s

In the 1920s, people started making plastic frames that could be shaped into any form.

Leopard glasses

Disco glasses

Star-shaped glasses

Superhero glasses

Halloween glasses

Glasses for hospital clowns

Almost invisible glasses

Glasses expressing an opinion

Night vision glasses for drivers

Glasses for noticeable characters

Dragonfly-shaped glasses

Glasses for lovers

Brick glasses

Glasses for dinosaur fans

Crocheted glasses

Futuristic glasses

HOW TO CHOOSE THE RIGHT GLASSES

It is very important for you to like the look of your glasses and find them comfortable. Only then you will wear them with pleasure and pride. Whereas the lenses are prescribed by the doctor based on a thorough check of your vision disorder, the shape, size, color, and material of the frame will be entirely up to you. Joe has chosen glasses with striped rims in his favorite colors. He likes to wear them every day. Kitty likes those glasses on Joe, but she would not feel right in such bold rims. However, she is considering getting another pair of glasses for special occasions — maybe with tiny silver stars?

These glasses on me? No way.

For the occasion

When trying on different glasses, you will probably consider your hair and eye color, as well as the shape of your face. You may be surprised how the same glasses look perfect on one person but totally wrong on another. This is because each of us has a unique face, and different shapes and colors suit different people. No wonder glasses are a true fashion accessory! Some people have several pairs of glasses at home, always picking a pair that matches their clothes or that they can wear for sports or as an adornment for theater.

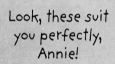

Look, these suit you perfectly, Annie!

Glasses for children

When Kitty was a little toddler, she wore different glasses than today. Glasses must perfectly fit the size of your face and the space between your eyes. If you choose them correctly, your glasses will never slip from your nose, even when you run about or jump up and down, and they will also never feel tight. Today, children's glasses are made of special resistant materials that are sufficiently robust but also light and flexible. You will just have to be careful not to break the frame — then you would have to get a new one, which is usually quite expensive.

FAMOUS VISUALLY IMPAIRED PEOPLE

Rosa Parks

Mahatma Gandhi

Benazir Bhutto

Elizabeth II

Famous athletes

Lydia Ko

Edgar Davids

Von Miller

Kareem Abdul-Jabbar

Meryl Streep

John Lennon

Woody Allen

Grace Kelly

Buddy Holly

Elton John

Groucho Marx

Famous film and music stars

18

Famous writers

Nikolai Gogol

Virginia Woolf

Charlotte Brontë

Ernest Hemingway

Famous visionaries and company founders

William Boeing

Steve Jobs

Bill Gates

Famous inventors and scientists

Katherine Johnson

Galileo Galilei

Grace Hopper

Stephen Hawking

Marie Curie

Famous painters

Rembrandt

Leonardo da Vinci

Claude Monet

Vincent van Gogh

GLASSES OF THE FUTURE

imagined by Joe
and Kitty

A A button to change the frame color (so that you can easily match the glasses with your clothes)

B A button for automatic cleaning

C A button for X-ray vision

D A button for fast translation of texts in foreign languages (the translation will appear in front of your eyes)

E Light for night vision

F Recording video-camera

G Camera controlled by blinking

H A projector screen for watching any video you wish

An end to eye defects

Thanks to the amazing progress in medicine, it is quite possible that soon doctors will be able to cure various eye defects easily and completely. Poor vision will be simply treatable. Doctors will detect babies' eye defects right after birth and treat them on the spot, while the babies will notice no discomfort.

Quick repairs

For adults, the vision check-up will take just a few seconds, and still be precise and accurate. All eye defects will be treated by a simple and painless laser operation. The patients will be able to go home immediately after the surgery.

Relaxed old age

Blind people will be able to see again, thanks to an artificial eye that will work just like the real one. Or perhaps even better! Old people will be able to read even the smallest letters without problems, and there will be a special gadget that will read a text out loud on request.

CHALLENGING DAYS

Sometimes wearing glasses can be a bit of a nuisance. Such as when ...

... it is raining, or someone points the garden hose at you.

... you come from outside into a warm room.

... you want to see a great movie in 3D.

... you are in a hot and humid environment, such as a sauna or a greenhouse.

... the sun is shining right into your eyes.

Clever helpers

But these little mishaps should not ruin your day. With a special spray and fine cloth, or special wet wipes, you can clean your glasses and see clearly within a few seconds.

Don't stop being active

Some sports, such as swimming or diving, are better done without glasses. Your glasses can wait in the safety of the case. But if you need to see perfectly even when doing such sports, you can buy special swimming or sports glasses, or even prescription sunglasses. With glasses, you can enjoy all the fun things that make a great day!

LOOKING AFTER OUR EYES

Even though some diseases, age, and family play an important role in eye defects, did you know that you can actually influence the future state of your eyes? Just as we need to look after our body to stay healthy, we must also take good care of our vision.

The benefits of sleep

Joe was very surprised to learn that in fact his eyes never sleep; they are always alert! When we are asleep, what rests are the eye muscles that help eyes move, as well as our eyelids. And they do deserve a lot of sound sleep.

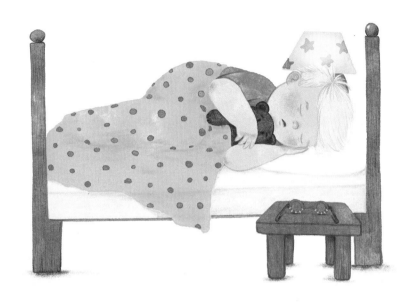

Dangerous sun

Sunshine can feel nice and warm on our skin, but parts of its light are harmful to us. That is why we should never forget to wear sunglasses with a good UV filter in summer. You can even buy special sunglasses for people with vision defects or special dark lenses that can be attached to your normal glasses.

You are what you eat

Everything we eat has an impact on our health. To have healthy eyes, you should eat fish, eggs, hazelnuts, or good vegetable oil. Yummy!

Useful exercise

When you feel your eyes are becoming tired or aching, you might try some of these exercises. They will surely bring you some relief!

Oh, those screens!

Kitty and Joe love watching cartoons together, but they know that looking at a TV, computer, or mobile phone screen for a long time is not good for their eyes. Eyes get tired from the artificial light, and since they tend to blink much less than they should when looking at a screen, they may start hurting, or may even become inflamed.

What else harms our eyes?

It's obvious that waving a stick in front of a friend's face is not a good idea. But you might be surprised that eyes also suffer from air-conditioning, which makes the air too dry, or from smoke and dust. Some people have more sensitive eyes than others, so they start feeling uncomfortable as soon as they enter an air-conditioned room.

1. Close your eyes and keep them shut for a few minutes. Will you be more patient than Joe?

2. Blink slowly and calmly. You can keep blinking in this way for a minute or so — just don't close your eyes too tightly.

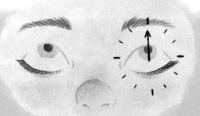

3. Close your eyes and imagine you are looking at a clock. Try to roll your eyes around the dial in one direction and the other with your eyelids still closed. Feeling better?

VISION IN THE ANIMAL KINGDOM

When visiting the zoo, the children discovered lots of exciting facts about different animals' vision. Did you know that...

Geckos have no eyelids, so they simply clean their eyes with their tongues. But they can see colors even in the dark!

A **dragonfly's** eyes, with thousands of lenses, cover most of its head. This helps the dragonfly see in all directions.

Tarsiers have huge eyes — the largest in proportion to the rest of the body among mammals. To reach the same proportion, human eyes would have to be the size of grapefruits!

Chameleons can control each eye separately. This enables them to look in different directions at once.

Unlike most other spiders, **jumping spiders** have excellent vision. With their two big front eyes they can see all the details, while the six smaller side eyes monitor every movement around them.

Camels protect their eyes from the sand, dust, and dry air of the desert with long eyelashes growing from both the top and the bottom eyelids. They also have a side lid, which they use to clean their eyes.

A **starfish** has something like eyes on the tips of its five arms. However, they can only distinguish light and darkness.

A fish called the **largescale four-eyes** looks as though it has, well, four eyes, but in fact it has just two. Each of them is split into two parts: the upper half looks above the water surface, while the bottom one checks what's going on underwater.

A **colossal squid** is the largest cephalopod in the world. Its eye is as big as a football!

Tiny crustaceans called **mantis shrimps** can see a vast number of colors, including those that are invisible to humans, such as ultraviolet or infrared. They can become invisible to other species while staying perfectly visible to their fellow mantis shrimps.

Snails can see, although with blurred vision, thanks to eyes placed on the tips of their nimble tentacles. This helps them look around without turning their whole body.

A **dog's** vision is not as extraordinary as its sense of smell or hearing, and since they can see only certain colors, such as green and yellow, their world is a lot less colorful than ours. For example, they can't see the color red at all!

The pupils of **cats** are not round but elliptical — a shape that lets much more light into their eye, helping cats see perfectly in the dark. Just like dogs, however, cats can't see the world in many bright colors like humans.

WE WEAR GLASSES — THAT'S FANTASTIC!

Glasses help you see all the details of our beautiful world!

Glasses look good on every face!

Glasses can emphasize your personality!

Joe has gradually found out that he and Kitty are not the only ones wearing glasses. He started noticing other people with glasses at the playgroup, on their block, in the street, and at shops; Kitty explained to him that even with glasses, he can do lots of exciting things.

At the beginning, Joe sometimes left his glasses on the bedside table, but later it happened less and less often, until one day he realized that he couldn't imagine life without his glasses. Don't worry, you too will get used to your glasses, and soon you'll become a proud, beautiful, and self-confident glasses-owner!

With or without glasses,
each of us is special and unique.
And that's great!

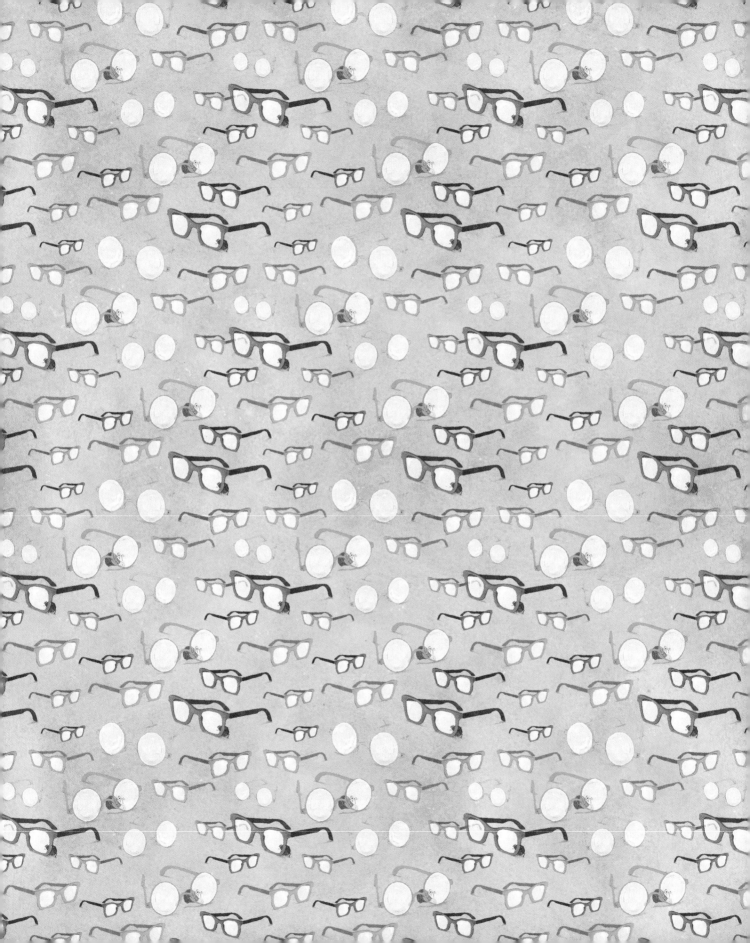